MY FATHER

Words and Music by Judy Collins

Pictures by Jane Dyer

Little, Brown and Company

Boston New York Toronto London

First Paperback Edition

Library of Congress Cataloging-in-Publication Data

Collins, Judy, 1939–
    My father/words and music by Judy Collins; pictures by Jane Dyer.
        p.   cm.
    Summary: A shared dream carries family members out of their drab life
into a finer world of music and travel, a dream later fulfilled by the youngest
daughter when she becomes a parent herself.

            ISBN 0-316-15228-5 (hc)
            ISBN 0-316-15238-2 (pb)

    1. Children's songs — United States. [1. Family life — Songs and music.
2. Parent and child — Songs and music. 3. Songs.] I. Dyer, Jane, ill. II. Title.
PZ8.3.C683My 1989
784.6′2405 — dc19   88-13945
                                                                   CIP
                                                                    AC

        10 9 8 7 6 5 4 3 2 1

                WOR

    Published simultaneously in Canada
    by Little, Brown & Company (Canada) Limited

    Printed in the United States of America

Paintings done in Luma dyes and colored pencils on 140-pound
Fabriano watercolor paper

My Father was written many years ago
and although my father never heard
the song, I have always felt that
the lyric made a spiritual connection
between my father and myself.

J.C.

For my father,
who shared his dreams.

J.D.

My Father

Words and Music by Judy Collins

Lyrically, nostalgic

fa-ther al-ways prom-ised us _____ that we ___ would live ___ in France. We'd go boat-ing

My father always promised us that we would live in France.

We'd go boating on the Seine

And I would learn to dance.

We lived in Ohio then;

He worked in the mines.

On his streams like boats we knew we'd sail in time.

All my sisters soon were gone to Denver and Cheyenne,

Marrying their grownup dreams, the lilacs and the man.

I stayed behind the youngest still, only danced alone,

The colors of my father's dreams faded without a sigh.

And I live in Paris now, my children dance and dream

Hearing the ways of a miner's life in words they've never seen.

I sail my memories of home like boats across the Seine,

And watch the Paris sun set in my father's eyes again.